ELECTRIC AFFINITIES

ELECTRIC AFFINITIES

MICHAEL PACEY

George Payerle, Editor

Cover design by Doowah Design.
Cover image by Karen Estabrooks.
Photo of Michael Pacey by Geoffrey Gammon.

"Dictionary" appeared in *Prairie Fire*; "Rubric" appeared in *Pottersfield Portfolio*; "Hawk and Handsaw" appeared in *The Malahat Review*; "Roots" appeared in *Qwerty*; "Light Bulb" and "Painters" appreared in *The Fiddlehead*; "Stovepipe" appeared in *The New Quarterly*; "Sunday Candy" appeared in *The Literary Review of Canada*; "Spirit Levels," "Provincial" and "Reading Shakespeare" appeared in *The Dalhousie Review*; "Nests" appeared in *The Antigonish Review*; "False Spring" and "Winter's Formality" appeared in the Salon section of *The Telegraph Journal.*

The author wishes to thank ArtsNB for funding this collection.

This book was printed on Ancient Forest Friendly paper.
Printed and bound in Canada by Hignell Book Printing Inc.

We acknowledge the support of The Canada Council for the Arts and the Manitoba Arts Council for our publishing program.

Library and Archives Canada Cataloguing in Publication

Pacey, Michael, 1952–, author
Electric affinities / Michael Pacey.

Poems.
ISBN 978-1-927426-66-1 (pbk.)

I. Title.

PS8581.A22E34 2015 C811'.54 C2015-901413-1

Signature Editions
P.O. Box 206, RPO Corydon, Winnipeg, Manitoba, R3M 3S7
www.signature-editions.com

for Nancy Bauer

CONTENTS

LIGHT BULB

Icon of pure idea. Screwed into a sphere of permanence
skin-thin, fragile as eggshell, yet suffused
with even light — a Platonic corona identical
to the thinking mind's delicate glow. Say,
above Henry's bulbous cartoon head, his second brain,
its single hair ablaze.

Naked, it suggests a folksy quality,
forever swinging its gaze
on unexpected corners of the past — corners lit
with the warm steady fire of your affection —
there was always one above your father
as you watched him work in basement or
garage (anywhere a bare bulb swings:
the genius of the place) — a galvanic presence overseeing
these Rembrandt-amber scenes, his hands tarred
with grease, the small tools kept separate and clean.

At the store — selecting the shade — *Arctic Pearl,*
Creamed Cumulus, Snow-Glare, inscribed
in tiny script round their poll — the wattage, frosted or clear
— the delicious sensation of walking out
as if you'd just bought bags of nothing,
cartons of air. Nestled inside
those egg-safe packets you coddle home
the power to see your rooms with the light
of still life. Screw a few in just for fun,
put the rest in a bowl: a bowl of glass pears.
Jars of sun. Tiny amphitheatres filled to the brim
with a thousand matinees.

Installation's easy — the global sign for "a dim bulb,"
— how many to construe those exaggerated threads?
Inside the candy-spun shell, tungsten filaments,

twin antennae yearn incandescent in a vacuum.
Your idea of home's within this soft white circuitry,
synapsing back and forth.

You catch its essence waking some morning
to find a light left on — see it up all night
worrying, keeping watch while you slept —
a conscience, consciousness. (You feel guilty.)
Giving the scene the third degree.
Like Picasso's *Guernica* — its single eye
witness to the nightmare below.

That moment when they expire:
you enter the room, flip the switch and Pop!
Apocalypse. Wick thins, disintegrates,
the globe grows cold, gray as rink-ice,
a dark rot spreads up the stem. Shake it:
you hear broken bits of distant music —
sleigh bells and pixie dust, then
a little click.

LIGHT BULB (II)

for Robert Gibbs

Quick tweaks
of the wrist —
in series — the Queen
waves like someone unscrewing
a burnt-out bulb.

Recalling Adam, reaching
to the Sistine ceiling
for a new bulb
to shed light on the scene below.
Illumination.

In overhead fixtures
you often find
a little nativity scene of flies,
beetles, moths —
their red eyes small glowing coals —
baked into a kind of
wakefulness.

Even Einstein, *the*
idea man, remains high-wattage
as if he's still plugged in, stuck
in a socket: his icon's taken on
that familiar bulbous shape —
shock of electric hair
just keeps growing,
strands raying out, like a cloud
of electrons,
moths orbiting a streetlight.

LIGHT BULB (III)

A string of metaphors
— in series —
make the page go
incandescent:
each likening
a 100-watt bulb
switched on

Like and unlike rubbing together,
the kindred and the incongruous
kindle resistance, the lines
start to crackle and hum —
the reader enters a state
of shock, riding the current
until the next surge
comes along. Neurons wired
high-voltage, entire brain
lit up like a bathroom.

SPIKE

Trying to recall a string of words —
every time I get close, there's
flutter, surge in the hum
of brain wattage; a rush, a spike
whipping the dials' needles
the way filings stand up,
charged with desire
when a magnet passes overhead.

Sensing its presence nearby —
"you're getting warm, warmer..."
but as I approach the nexus,
niche where its lodged white-
hot like a splinter in your finger,
the force-field switches poles,
resistance pushes me away.

I circle back, swinging in
from different directions four or
five times, then dive straight
through this node of static, nest
of interference, and find
the mislaid words,
lost message,
illumination.

SPIRIT LEVELS

are best approached obliquely.
Like oracles.

To enter that free-floating, evenly-
suspended state required in fine
carpentry, pause for a moment...
staring blankly at a level
balanced in your hands.

Peer into its vials of colored alcohol
(inventor Thévenot
preferred a good red) until
its irises, two gulps of air,
see eye to eye inside,
resting on tiny horizons.

Squint. Tilt your head. And
hope
for the best. Truth
is like a hammer.
A level is more like hope.

HAWK AND HANDSAW

"I know a hawk from a handsaw."
— Hamlet

Cold blue of the blade
hanging on its peg — metallic blue
of tools — steel teeth
tell of origins: some carnivore's
long jawbone.

The bird hooded, strung with
jesses, strops its beak and
spreads its wings;
right hand on the saw's grip,
left thumbnail guides the cut —
index of desire
sure as hawk and handler.

A stroke/swoop:
the wood below still, yet swaying
in a wide slow rhythm, pine
or spruce; a quick divide — the
narrow kerf,
sudden puff of dust.

The hawk's perch is called a *block.*
Fine cuts are said to be *feathered.*
The blade is called *evening calm.*

SNARE

Their ways written in
the little runs they make, back
and forth to their lair; no need to sit
and wait — look at the grass
bent down, bruised, brushed aside —
a trail.

Take a length of string or wire,
anything supple yet strong; weave
a slip knot noose at one end, the tail
suspend from a branch along the run.

He'll never see it — the mouth
of a dark sack above his worn groove —
until, in a cinch, it's measured his neck.
He keeps his blind spot dead ahead
(if only he'd look *to one side*).

He'd shake his head ruefully,
if he could; too late
for being awake to make
any difference.

CARPENTERS

wrote their names somewhere
inside your house —
with a pencil, nail, piece of chalk —
maybe a stick or finger
stuck in mortar.

On the backs of bricks in the fireplace,
behind the mantelpiece —
under the eaves where you sleep.
On the underside of rafters.
Joists.

On the spine of your house —
the other side, hidden side —
the men who framed and made it,
paused
to sign it.

PAINTERS

Piebald, thin as ladders, perpetually
lightheaded (the many years
of inhaling solvents); men of surfaces,
of bristled allegiances:
varsol versus turpentine,
heat-gun or scraper.
Each has *his* way of making paint
adhere to wood. Prone to squabbles —
best left to work alone, or in uneasy pairs.

A wife who left long ago.

The fickleness of paint.

Their nemesis: troops of students
who roll into town each summer
brandishing spray guns,
slapping on paint with 20-foot rollers;
discussing the weekend
during long breaks beneath the trees.

A painter never takes vacations;
wherever he'd go, he'd see
drips, flakes, jaded pigment:
a world in need of one more coat.

His holidays are rain.

ROOTS

Under each tree,
a second set of branches
reaches out, seeking damp earth
instead of the warm-hearted sun,
longing for its dark
disconsolately.

Blind, feeling their way
through the dirt, they drink
slowly from underground streams,
scour rocks and bones
they encounter — long nights
of grief their day.

This side of the tree needs
to be alone below the loud
green canopy. In endless winter
limbs bend when no winds blow,
cradle only rueful fruit:
handfuls of polished stones.

CROWN

A storm approaches. You
decide to go for a walk, but
what you want to do is climb
into the crown of the largest tree
in the yard, rising through
green levels smoothly as if on
an escalator, carrying various
stringed instruments: guitar,
violin, maybe bow and arrow,
and seated in a fork, begin to strum
and sing as the winds pluck you.

Riding your instruments like
horses, you'll turn
through the skies, rain staccato
on skin, trees all
nodding their heads and
no one passing underneath
can see you there — this small
green music — because you're
gone on a long journey, long gone,
no, those below could see only
branches galloping overhead,
leaves gonging madly.

SAW AND TREE

The small teeth of the saw
telling the large tree
what to do, when to die.
And how. Why.

The saw whispering away
down there, chattering away,
consoling it; some say,
regaling the tree with old proverbs.

MEMORY TREE

Waking. A memory comes to me — one of those
you recall every decade or so, rising
to the surface for reasons of its own.

A huge elm used to stand at the intersection
of the sidewalk and our driveway, just this side
of the public sphere and the strip of concrete
ruled by our Ford Monarch. Testifying
to its ancient nature, it crowned
other trees in the neighborhood,
and its bark like wrinkled elephant hide
bore many scars. I stared up
as the elm swayed in a strong wind, and sang
a kind of whale music back to it.

Meeting place, *home* in hide-and-seek, at its base
we set squashed bouquets of wildflowers — violets
and daisies gathered for our mother.
But what set this large tree apart: a series
of ornate niches and cubbyholes,
nooks and hollows.

Here we'd place backyard finds
like molten shards of sea-glass,
mottled stones, feathers, handmade nails and
pieces of broken porcelain;
offerings of forget-me-not and bloodroot.
And we made shrines for dead birds.

All the kids on Winslow would drop by —
even passersby, the mailman,
could be seen pausing
to read the signs, drop off a flyer or
hand-written Hello. An alternative mailbox.

Eventually younger kids took over —
but I'd still come, find mementos
of stones or fragments of colored glass.
When I went away to college the town fathers
decided all elms must be destroyed —
a plague of tiny beetles eating away their insides.
Men with ropes and chainsaws cut it down,
cut it up and carted its trunk and limbs away.

They filled the hole and planted grass, but
there's still a large hollow, or network of hollows
down there, where the roots of the elm
slowly decay — because every heavy rain
all the water drains away down there.
Grottoes branching off
into the dark soil.

And I know these caverns are down there
below the front lawn, subterranean,
because every ten or twenty years
bits of those icons come back,
the little leaves, twigs, blossoms of the Memory Tree.

CUP

Vowel's deep bowl,
dark well —
steep sides solid consonants.

The *U*
a tiny cup and handle.

Utensil modeled on your palms
cupped — fingers wattled tight.
A tool for gripping liquids.

Put away in the *cupboard,*
obscured, you
hear only half the word.

Take it out, fill it to the brim.
Carry to your corner, sip
by sip commune —
you and tea slowly merging —
each cup holds one ocean.

PANTRY

I lead them through the kitchen and
pause at the pantry, where the girl
begins to coo, so I say,
"I love pantries," and the guy
gets embarrassed, as if I'd said
"I love panties," but she's moved in-
side, caressing the doll-sized shelves,
paper-lined, taking deep breaths —
"this is exactly how my granny's pantry
smells," turning round and round
picturing this shrine to gods of food
all ginger and cinnamon,
mmmmm,
and cupcakes with pink frosting.

Now she's opening
small drawers and cupboards,
plotting where she'll place preserves,
jams, jellies, pickles, her
cookie jar and donut tins, muttering —
even his face is glazed with that
"can I have a cookie?" look and
what she whispers next is,
"we'll take the place."

SUNDAY CANDY

Those mornings in bed you pray
somehow they'll let you stay home:
then you think of the moment
Sunday school ends, those fifteen minutes
before the grown-ups sing their final hymn —
how you'll run across the street
to the tiny candy-store (there's one
across from every church)
and give half the offering your father
pressed into your hand
to the old agnostic behind the counter.

This is money for God.
But your religion's the faith of candy —
so you give it to the old man still
in his slippers and bathrobe.
Miraculously, each weekend, this
second allowance has arrived:
you've made a choice, stolen half
the tithe, now stand pointing out
chocolates and licorice
behind finger-smudged sheets of glass.
He crams them in a small brown paper bag.

You cram them down your gullet
before the long ride home.

Riding a sugar-rush all the way,
a delicious ride home from church:
in the back seat,
the blood in your veins
thickly renewed, and yes, yes,
riding the sweet rapture of sin.

PUCK

for Richard

Clearing the garden beds each spring,
I harvest a half-bucket of
hockey pucks —
shot wide of the net
from Sheppard's backyard rink.

Heavy, enigmatic discs.
Periods. Dots.
Marks at the end of a sentence.

Some say its name comes from German *punkt,*
for point, dot; or Irish *poc,* to poke or punch.
Or *origin unknown.*
Some from *Puck,*
sprite of mischievous ways.

Tricks: versus a ball, its flight
cannot be projected, say, on its edge;
goalies often fooled, goalies
unpredictable too: streaky, up, down,
all over the place (I've always felt sorry
for goalies), flailing away
as the Vulcanized biscuit glides upstairs
where mom keeps the peanut-butter
cookies.

I have a friend, a former goalie,
whose bucket list ends with this wish:
his ashes, dyed black,
be compressed into a hockey puck
and dropped — not into the cold, gray earth
— but at centre ice, Canada Cup.

Not the showy opening face-off though —
he wants to be *in* the game —
beginning of Overtime. Sudden death.

DISHRAG

Wringing its cloth hands
all day long, weeping
into the kitchen sink, addled
with bacteria; a fetish
beneath the faucet —
again and again its worn teats
pulled — the water comes back
milky white
long before it runs clear
through threadbare fibers.

Mother grabbed this very rag
to scour the crust around your mouth
— all the way to school tasting
despondency of stagnant ponds
— dishrag's raw contagious kiss.

A BREEZE CALLED MARY

The fall I'm five, Mom
walks to school with me —
second day,
I have to learn to go alone —
"But I'll always be there,
coaxing your feet."

So I set off:
second block, a breeze
arrives, stirring fallen leaves,
coaxing my feet —
I look about —
know it is her.

Several falls later, a song
on the radio underlines her identity:
"They Call the Wind Mariah."
A few more,
Hendrix whispers
"The Wind Cries Mary."

A gentle breeze always feels
motherly to me.

STAIRS

Stairs became her downfall:
nearly blind, she fights now to turn
back, turn back each time we
approach that dark chute:
risers and treads
pouring down
like a mountain cataract —
white-capped rapids'
troughs and crests —
a dark whirlpool.

Blindness made her see
more clearly
this creaking, crooked device —
most dangerous tool
we keep in the house.

MIRRORS

Mirrors are windows turned inside-out,
windows turned inwards.
That's why they make rooms larger.

Mirrors are pieces of a slow-moving stream
that winds its way through your house:
past the sink, over the bureau —
waterfall of drawers.

Mirrors are always concentrating, trying
to memorize each detail: the comb's
sly spine,
its smile of teeth.

Sometimes you find yourself wandering
around at night, checking to see
if you remembered to turn off the lights,
if the mirrors still remember your face.

CLOTHES-HANGER

bare suggestion of human,
mannequin *manqué*:   yard of
iron wire bent — sloped shoulders
pair of arms folded — ends rat-
tail twisted spliced   then
finished off with a fish-hook
for a head.
a device to wear your clothes
while you wear something else.
stripped: loss, the lostness
of each of us.
ghosts of long-dead valets.

two or three were here, left
behind, when you first moved in —
swinging open the closet
your arm brushed against them —
they struck up a music atonal and
strange, a suite for rusty triangles.

your welcoming committee.

SHOES

Gutting this house
I kept finding black shoes
hid behind laths and plaster,
placed, side by side, atop sills
in the basement: "concealments,
concealment shoes,"
to kick away the winged ones.

First they used ancestors,
then their feet.
Then, shoes.

We bury old boots
to keep snakes out of gardens,
throw them at those just married.

Smooth and shiny,
they slowly look like you:
frowning, wrinkled, toes
and tongues curled up,
heels ground down —
so much *us* in our shoes.

How you carry your body.
Your walk.

Searching for books
in second-hand stores, I'm
drawn unaware
to the footwear section —
feel an urge
to touch worn leather.

Our feet know us, know
the earth in ways we won't.
Our sorrows seep into our shoes,
working their way
to those worn heels.

GUEST SOAP

A jar of guest soap in the bathroom
you were taught *not* to use —
"*just for guests.*" But even guests
were afraid to use it. Preserved
here for forty years. Little cakes
of soap shaped like blown roses —
like those miniature roses you pinned
on your girl the night of the mini-prom
back in junior high.
"Sweetheart roses."
Cakes preserved side by side like
husbands and wives
tucked into their beds, each determined
not to be the first to die. Soap
you could never buy in any store
("*not available in stores*")
given to your mom at Christmastime
from someone in some other country
like that wire-mesh tin lamp shaped
like a sailing-ship a student from India
gave your Dad that blew up
every time he tried to plug it in.
(Back then all the wires around the world
spoke their own code). Small cakes
of soap with all the gold paint flaked
off now, a sour green inside, preserved
like a baby in a jar of alcohol, small curls
of milky amniotic fluid snaking
up from the bottom.

Or no, more like those ancient jars of pomade
and brilliantine lined up beneath the mirror
at Harry Nixon's shop — those murky
vessels no one would *ever* choose
to splurge on —
all your friends went with a dollar

down to Fox's right on Queen
but your father always sent you
to Harry's place, size of a bathroom or
a cage for animals on a grubby backstreet,
fifty cents in your pocket:
Harry would do the job for that.
Next day your friends would cry,
"Your barber's a bootlegger!" and yes
the very next time amidst the snipping
and buzzing, a pal of Harry's walks in,
sporty and jovial, so Harry presses your head
down as if he's about to start on the back
of your neck, but you swivel your eyes
from the jars of pomade up to the mirror
instead. Harry hands him a bottle
wrapped in a brown paper bag.
After he left Harry said, "I don't really do that
anymore; just a favour for an old friend ..."
Years later studying Chaucer
in freshman English, you're not at all
shocked when the prof tells the class
barbers used to double as early surgeons:
if you needed something — a nose or
limb — cut off or maybe stuck back on
just turn in at the pole with a white bandage
all gored in blood wound around it,
and your moonlighting barber
will do the job. And just
for good luck, mix up a poultice or
pour a palm's-worth of goo from a jar
just like this, and slap it
on that lump on the back of your neck.

SCISSORS

Perpetually plural:
twin sisters fastened together —
their incest the fencing
of two naked blades.

A bad conjunction.

Their hinged jaws meet: the sound the sea makes,
the sound of two knives
in love (fused at the hips, groins piston in sync).
Your hands run on — thumb and index gripped
in steel stirrups — can't stop
cutting paper into strips,
docking the curtains, pruning your eyebrows,
the wiring, pinking your hair —
pixillated as a seamstress.

A man with two wives: one side of their
seesaw shark-faced smile whispers sssh sssh sssh
while the other one goes snip snip snip....

BROOM

Old broom worrying the dirt
out from the corners
coaxing it
out into the light;
its frayed straw
can't fail to see the irony
in this sour harvest:
tiny haycocks/
stooks of crumbs and dust.

Now you must proffer
the absurd little pan —
grip its effete "milady" handle
and bow down
before what you made:
small mounds of ennui.

PINING

Sombre pines: wind in
their branches — the sound
of grieving, bereavement.
To pine: to grow thin with
longing, to mourn. To
pine for one long gone,
to grow long and thin.
Needles aligned in
fan-shaped bunches,
small brushes whisking
the air: a whisper
(sighing/soughing).

Sound of a broom
consoling the floor; the
sound a teakettle makes —
water rousing to a boil —
a plume of steam rising.

COCOONS

Pale green cocoons
on the shady side of the house
each September, moored with thread
to the clapboards, tucked
under the ridge
where the boards clap together.

A sleeper lies in state inside
each small hammock,
swaddled in filaments fine
as dental floss or muslin —
waiting, wintering over
before spring's flight.

Picture her through gauze,
cocoon, cozy boudoir:
for five days and nights, weaving
the dress she wears — she becomes
a spindle, whirling, disappearing
as she spins — each gown or shroud
one size smaller. Layer
by layer, withdrawing inside
her wardrobe, she seals both ends
of her craft, coffin.
Then egg-shaped sleep.

GLUE

When the oceans receded and land first appeared,
great sloughs and pits of glue
pocked the surface of the globe:
the Sahara, a landlocked viscous sea,
Australia a vast honeypot.
Huge lagoons round the Tortugas.
Evaporation made surfaces, once wet,
increasingly sticky. Single-celled creatures
glommed together; globs and globules —
the great age of Glomming On had begun.
Glue circulated, fell like rain from
ropy spiral clouds, in which asteroids
and small planets became ensnared,
long rancid butter-colored strips that turned slowly
overhead. Everything became clingy,
tacky, even the air —
the sun turned away in disgust.
(Hid behind a yellow cloud.)

A map of these times (or for that matter,
a map of Time) would have to be made of glue
in long sheets shellacked and overlaid, with
little loops of hardened material — elastics —
floating about on top.
To suggest longitude.

The darkness lifted: attitudes hardened,
relations became brittle;
the great glue-pits had disappeared —
eventually replaced by pitch-pots,
boiled horse-hooves, mucilage, syrup.

But the glue-pits hadn't dried up — they simply
seeped down into the centre of the Earth —
our core a molten ball of glue,
waiting. Agglomerating.

GLUE (PART 2)

a thank you to Bartholomew Angelicus

In ancient days they named a body of water
Lake Asphaltus; due to its solemn mood
it was also called the Dead Sea.
For beneath its waves
nothing could live or breathe; and
when you tried to drown any creature,
fish or fowl — soon as thrust down,
it smote the surface again.

And the waters didn't move with the wind,
lying flat and still in all weather.
And no ship rows or sails on this sea, because
anything lifeless sinks to the bottom.
So unlit lanterns drown; lit ones float like buoys.

At night this lake casts up black clots of glue,
in the brim whereof trees grow
whose apples stay green when ripe.
Cut open, you find ashes inside.
Men journey to these sad shores
only to chew one piece of this burnt fruit,
to down a mouthful of this brackish glue.
O sticky pilgrims!

For they say, during the long night that follows
you'll speak with the dead;
and once their words
enter your ears
for the rest of your days your thoughts cohere
with the pure idea of glue.

HOW PLUTO MUST FEEL

Deposed planet… Cast out,
dragged through Space,
disconsolate.

In every set, an anomaly:
thumb, black, zero — in time
thrust aside to the margins,
found out. See Newton's *Principia*:
the forces of attraction and repulsion
a matched pair, poised;
it takes so little — glitch, short circuit
to throw the switch.

How Pluto must feel — talk about
comeuppance — blithely pursuing
its orbit; then bounced, banished.
Shed.
A lump that tried to glom on,
glob in a grey galaxy
of nameless globs of ice.
Scruff.

Shoved around the dimly lit universe
like a grocery cart in a parking lot,
wheels gummed up with slush —
a thin endless drizzle —
cheesy satellites blinking on &
off in the distance, like neon.

BREAKING A SNAKE

Something slides out of the ditch
and under my wheels —
faster than thought
I hit the brakes
look in the rearview mirror,
shudder, and hit the gas.

The snake's writhing back there
like a broken fan belt,
smashing himself against the asphalt,
as if to shed not just his skin —
but his head, the road itself —
that carries me calmly on.

NUTHATCH, YARROW, LOUSE

In Japan, shi means both poem *and* poetry;
it also denotes nuthatch, yarrow, *and* louse.

i.

Restless, nuthatch scrambles up and
down the long-limbed trees —
short droll legs, big tenacious feet —
never stops trying to find
what's hidden in plain sight — treasure
in the trunk's sly crevices: seeds,
larvae, and best, this: another tough nut
to crack, hacking away at it for hours,
"hatching" it with his deft beak, equally
at home upside-down, blood
singing to his head.

ii.

Walk by any roadside — fixed
in ditches, old fields, waste places —
here comes old flat-top, a headful
of medicine: tight clusters
of tiny disc-flowers, *yarrow,* or *milfoil.*
Achilles found yarrow growing beside
the battlefields of Troy — brewed it to staunch
his warriors' wounds; more lore
nodding Homer forgot to stick in his book.

It heals the tongue: Saxons steeped
the leaves to cure stutterers,
the Malicite the mute. A tonic no one turns
to now — persistent, a pest
among suburban lawns. Raw stink:
sneezeweed, even the nose turns up at,
turns down.

iii.

At least louse *knows* he's not wanted —
eternal stowaway, hiding is
his every thought, blood his destination.
The body sways around him
like a long-limbed forest, the body
surrounds him like a large pungent flower.

Listen: you can almost hear him hum —
he's found a fresh vein to tap
and he's working it — at peace
in his bloodbath, his physic — drawing off
the red milk he will never be weaned of;
it's life itself
he can't live without.

NESTS

1. Pillowstuffs: tufts of rabbit's-foot clover,
milkweed silk, and dandelion down, combed
and thumbed, molded into a thimble
tied together, tied down, with spider's silk,
saddle-wise, to a forked limb,
or nestled among the needles of white pine–
home — the only place a hummingbird's
unblurred, at rest.

2. Well-worn hammock, cradle,
the oriole's familiar metaphor —
the domestic scene hanging by a thread,
dependants depending from the utmost tips
of willows, elms; a text, an itchy pouch
a purse woven of grasses, bark and string.

3. A wren prefers similes, body mimicry–
small holes or crannies, smocked with leaves and
feathers: coat pockets, tin cans,
a mailbox. First makes a series of drafts,
"dummies," cast off and cast aside,
until a certain arrangement of materials
falls into place, fits a figure within.

4. Slipshod wicker picnic basket, packed
with reeds, matted hair, shiny things — tinfoil, lures,
lost keys — whatever the crow's coveted, picked up;
to be appraised in the glow
of the moon's borrowing.

5. Slowly, the swift hatches a saucer
of sticks, padded with moss and wool,
licks the dish till it's glazed like crockery;
then with spittle, sticks it to the face of a cliff.

Whatever's been picked up, borrowed, found,
I gather together, surround, pat down —
a construction makeshift,
gluey strings of words moved around,
the template inside; held in place, stuck with sweat,
with spit, to the sheer edge of a page.

READING SHAKESPEARE

We learned to read each scene, set
on a bare wooden stage, in school;
at night I'd add my inner geography,
each assigned page would unfold
in the woods where I used to play.

Even now, gathering fiddleheads,
walking the dog by the river,
recognize the spot where Ophelia descends
the stairway of her stream; witches sit
in the old graveyard, cooking up stew.
Turn to the ordinary Saint John, see instead,
Cleopatra's barge burn on the waters,
Prospero abandon ship.

Reading Shakespeare, all the scenes filmed
in deft locations here by the river, as if
scouted in advance. And watching the action,
I see superimposed the ground down here
two or three feet in the air, just hovering;
see the earth and grass and wildflowers,
close-up, and somehow *lyrically*.

Unaware, I chose this spot, and not
surprisingly: because of its history,
this is where the town's founders spent
their first cruel winter — many lie buried
on the knoll I use in Hamlet's opening act;
and because they were Loyalists, loyal
to England's queen.
So this is Shakespeare's place, for me:
a small wild place, set off on its own,
compact, varied; a place impossibly
green.

TENNYSON'S BROTHERS

All had Dad's mould to pour
their bottomless melancholy in;
Arthur was partial to gin, or vodka.
Or rum. Fred preferred Mozart —
hired violins by his villa windows
so he'd waken to Wolfgang —
some mornings instead of listening,
he sits and looks at his wrists.
Charles came down from Cambridge
magna cum laudanum. Poor Ed,
full of woe — woke one morning,
weeping. Sixty years on, he
wouldn't stop. Horatio still had
far to go — *wee wee wee*
all the way home to mommy's house.
The seventh rose from his sprawl
on the carpet to greet Rossetti,
"I am Septimus,
most morbid of the Tennysons."

A stain in the genes; all the sons
enact the grim ritual
of Dad's last days: the many ways
of welcoming death.
Even Queen Vic
was sparking fat spliffs
to "ease my cramps," she claimed.

Of all the fruit-about-to-turn
hanging from the family tree,
it was Ed Alfred felt closest to.
It's said they always understood
each other: boyhood codes, secrets,

then the break — Ed's departure,
treason, first and deepest —
one night
his brother closed his eyes and veered
off like a comet, on his own dark orbit.

TENNYSON'S PENUMBRA

With age, the urge to cast
a large shadow,
to put on that hat put off so often.

Like Tennyson, towards the end,
showing up everywhere
in an enormous black sombrero.

ESCALATOR DOWN

One day a package arrived
addressed to my dad — the back
of the manila envelope, as well as
the blank covers of the slim volume inside,
Escalator Down, smeared with lines of furious prose.
It turned out one of my father's ex-students
had sent this poisoned epistle
and self-published novel
as a kind of revenge, crowded words
illustrating its front more luridly
than any paperback hack could.

Escalator Down: a man descends an escalator
to a subway station; his ticket,
or rather, handful of tokens, takes him to visit
one by one the women he has hurt.
Gradually, reader and protagonist realize
his death occurred just before
the text's first words — his descent
to the underworld. To this hell for men
who've hurt women, torn apart their lives.

Did the author somehow suss my father's story?
Was this embittered hothead/dropout in fact
a seer, a genius, his feeble masterwork more
than mere vengeance on an arrogant prof?

Dad caught me reading it — as his son, of course
I couldn't tear myself away.
What did I think? "Intermittently amusing,"
I replied. He snorted his derision.
Where's that book now? Lost in the
basement floods? Thrown out?
Burnt?

Dad liked to burn things in the fireplace,
or else the backyard. I saw him reading
Escalator Down
out in the garden one afternoon.

Sometimes at night we walk in Hell together —
Dad's blind now, but I can still see.
Virgil and Dante? Hardly.
We're lowly workers here,
whispering in circles as we tend
to the women we've hurt — visiting them
repeatedly. No chance of moving on.

WATERGATE

The lawn turned brown that summer
despite the sprinkler's worst intentions;
my father would come home from work
— slam the red door of his Mustang —
complaining of the heat. Each evening
we'd watch the men testifying
to their sordid crimes, sweating
in the gaze of our television sets —
Haldeman Erlichman Dean — like the
parade of names you gradually become
familiar with at a party. The heat
and stale air of summer; behind it all,
the sense of an unseen worm, larva-white,
a pale grub twisting in its own juice.

As if a seedy old planet had
swum into view.
We sat in the living room
night after night
waiting for all the fathers to confess.

KITCHEN TABLE

Kitchen table, long ago
carried upstairs to this back room
as the family, crowded around,
multiplied to nine. My sleek Mac
on its worn wooden surface.

Pens, pencils, notes, drafts
have replaced salt and pepper,
cups and plates;
the clatter, laughter, fights
exchanged for the soft rain
of my keypad
forming messages.
Words I try out loud, grace.

At this table where my mother set
another warm meal each night,
I take my daily bread,
another piece of paper.

J. B.'S AUTO-ICONS

Bentham was a born hoarder — putting
everything to good use, his god.
Said the dead shouldn't be prodigally
shoveled under, but, suitably lacquered,
put out to pasture as lawn jockeys.
What need a coat of arms nailed to the gate,
when your antecedents gauntlet the drive?
If a country gentleman has rows of trees
leading to his dwelling,
the auto-icons of his family might alternate...

Why *do* we let the dead squander their days
catching up on their correspondence,
trying to forgive eneryone —
when they could be turned to account
as mannequins, *memento mori;*
taught to pull their own weight
at a series of part-time jobs: grandad, candied —
sentry, tailor's dummy, or dime-store santa claus;
parents, uncles, aunts, amply shellacked
and *abracadabra* —
night watchmen, scarecrows, traffic cops.
That sickly niece who just sighed her last,
glazed, and to a ship's prow lashed.
A copal varnish would protect the face
from the effects of rain;
caoutchouc the habiliments.

Tongue-in-cheek, you chortle? A philosopher
pulling the dependable tail? Check out his
bequest, lodged in the foyer at University College:
Jeremy's jury-rigged remains.
But, as the sign says, *please* —
don't use the sage's outstretched palm
to extinguish your cigarette.

DEATH OF A POET

When his friends brought the body downstairs
and out to a waiting car,
they said his weight was like a feather
— perhaps the world had become heavier.
Perhaps they could sense
the buoyancy of his last rhetoric.
Perhaps it was the whiskey.
They agreed there was a contradiction
in heft, in mass, nevertheless.

Like the difference between an old house
you pass every day — suddenly torn down,
destroyed — and its foundation,
impossibly small. Even the lot
is more, but less;
instead of spacious and free,
looks fenced-in and insignificant
when those rooms
the carpenters invented out of the air
have disappeared.

A contradiction in terms, in tense —
the poet dying, his body and
the body of work: the long poems
that appeared on his horizon
towards the end
like three-masted craft in full sail,
fabulous as tall ships,
just papers stuffed in a bottle now,
messages,
pages in a little-read book.

(His friends all bought a copy,
but even his friends he had to press.)

DICTIONARY

i. Sometimes the *right* word eludes you
rounding corners, you can taste its scent in the air
on the sharp point of your tongue,
where nouns and verbs are born.
Search through thesauri, reverse dictionaries,
query old friends, until once again
you realize there is no such word:
no word for that loamy odour only knees exude;
no word for those insignificant streetscapes,
a certain intersection say, that play in your head,
thinking of something else;
no word for the sound the pinetops make.

There are many more, of course —
ghost words one might call them,
except they're the opposites of ghosts.

ii. I've always felt sorry for words on their way out,
words whose only currency is cached
in a single phrase — *eke, vim, kibosh,*
kaboodle. Words overdrawn, in fact,
phrases only a grandfather
would try to use as money:
hornswoggle, pang, jiffy, jink.
In dictionaries their lineage reads "origin unknown"
but actually they're Lamarck's children,
picking their way across the face of the earth,
thundering herds overhead,
their semi-transparent skeletons exposed to the air.

iii. Despite years disciplining freshman text,
certain words I misspell myself —
not those mis-struck/lucky typos,
the English loanguage, Canadian litterature,
but consistently wrong in longhand:
arguement — because it takes
all the sting out of your attack to diminish the verb;
develope — because that's the only way
the process feels complete to me.
Orthography is oligarchy.

iv. Last, the words you dial up repeatedly
in the dictionary, but the next time you meet,
a year later or even a few weeks,
you can't recall their name,
insist they're someone else: *caryatid,* for example,
a small South American beetle
that flies through the trees at night;
quincunx, a bitter green fruit full of large seeds;
and an *impetigo,* an Andalusian bird
said to have the most beautiful song of all.
These are the words that belong to you,
forced to wear a disguise in the world —
but no one can take them away from you.

K

"I find the letter K offensive,
almost nauseating."
— Kafka

K stalks dim corridors of text — some
seedy Eastern European font, some
regime of print,
punch-cut type — crowded paragraphs
with no place to stop and rest, his
two legs always walking, his
arms outstretched, out of place
in alphabet's labyrinth, tight alleys
and winding streets of sign.

(one day you wake, and
I = K, and
K = X).

I

Roman column —
one capital letter
holding up the world —
devouring
all the other letters —
first person imperious,
Adam down
to you or I.

I'm writing a kind of
autobiography — with
all the parts about me
cut out —
every I excised.

MIDDLE LETTER

A child in the dentist's chair,
I'd anesthetize myself
by staring at the words
on the building across the street:
Federal Offices. I'd find
the central letter of each,
e and *i*,
and switch my attention
from one to the other.

Now, during crises:
arguments, car accidents, surgery,
I catch myself taking a word,
inamoratu, say, repeating it,
then determining the middle letter,
focusing on it.

As if, all along I sensed
words could help me out of this,
pull me through.

M/N

"By the side of one stand the Muses and Memory,
beside the other oblivion and silence; the other is
the lord of unseeing Night."
— Plutarch, "On the E at Delphi."

M, in the middle, at the edge of the divide, break, slide —
M in media res, sign of water, of the sea, of the oasis.
Of all things, water's best — softest, most yielding —
mmmm the small round heads of shaggy waves: start
writing a series of m's, and your hand wants to keep on,
right out to sea. Or MMMM, whitecaps bristling with capitals.
Source of Life. First home. Deliverer from thirst.
Mother/maman/ma/mater/mere/madar/matka/moder/
madre/mutter/mai. And mer the sea, and moon.
And M for Memory.

But next, N for No and Night; N sign of the snake —
of the infinite negative, raised to the nth power.
M and N side by side, strange alphabet-fellows —
the two nasals: twins near identical in sound, sign.
Two sides of the fault line, the crack before Q, quagmire
of U/V/W, horror of XYZ. On one side: NoNoNoNoNo;
on the other, drowning it out, an interminable hum,
the ocean's murmur, mmmmmmmmmmmmmmmmmm.

Y

Y, an old tree
beside a road
also the road itself—
where it forks.
A great river
dividing, converging.
A man
with his hands to the sky.

Y is always the meeting,
and Y
the parting ways.

RUBRIC

Deep in Dickens' *Bleak House*,
I turn 263 over to 4;
there at the head of the page
pressed between the leaves
like a pansy or maple leaf—
snaring the eye like italics
or parentheses — the exoskeleton
of a centipede, each appendage
spelled out as in an insignia
or signature, delicate as Cyrillic font.
His characteristics
preserved in detailed portraiture,
19th-century grotesquerie.

Late at night — flicking back and forth —
my eyes play tricks:
the legs begin to twitch,
centipede enters the text,
devious, full of tics.
Up Holborn Hill,
the heroine hears
hundreds of footsteps,
meticulous pursuit.

FOUND POEM AND A COMMENTARY

i.

The Mercury, Fredericton, NB
December 26, 1826:
To the Editor, Sir, I beg leave to inform
my friends and the public
I have imported from Rotterdam
a portable hand-mill for making Poetry;
this mill, acting upon
revolving polished cylinders
is fit for Pathetic or Love sonnets.
Also, a mill propelled by horse power,
adapted for Prose:
Abstruse or Stubborn Subjects.

ii.

Tumblers tumble, the sleek mill purrs —
words in combinations innumerable:
the prosody of polished cylinders.
Bard-in-a-Box, imported *and* portable,
strapped to your back, spun by hand,
hand in hand with the hand of chance;
automatic, it deals out, octet and
sestet, in nimble enjambment, feet that dance.

For those who prefer prose — leaden, pedestrian, mechanical —
set the dial for Stubborn, Abstruse, or just plain Dull.
As you trudge to the edge of the page, and back, stuck in a rut,
whipped in blind circles, on a wheezing, fly-blown horse,
pause every few paces to drop a *Thus*, an *Albeit*, a *But*,
a *Nevertheless*, an *Of course, of course, of course.*

PROVINCIAL

Backedup backwater
bumfuck newbrunswick
backdoor to the front-
ier (Upper C's
treasure chest);
upside hills and backwash
waterfalls.
Nova Scotia's ugly sister.
And daughter (family
compacted: isthmus umbilicus).
Ass backwards ripped
from her ribs.

But n.b. (note well):
her emerald body
            (all pockets and
                        soft peaks).
Once one rose in the house
and said, Let's call her New
Ireland, for side by side
in Pangaea, before the continents
were torn apart
(pair packed in peat)
cheek by cheek.

"No," the call came back.
We'll honour the German home
of England's Queen.
(Not, let's say, *White Pineland*
for here the great ghosts
gone as masts in her fleet;
or *Schoonera*, for here the cradle
that vanquished France.)

"No," the call came back.
Then some wag said,
"Let's put a Spanish galleon on
the flag."

RAMPS

Like sailors beaching their craft,
as darkness falls
boys drag their makeshift ramps
up from the pavement
onto neighbouring lawns —
homemade launch pads fashioned
from pallets, fenceposts, picnic tables, sleds;
a hodgepodge scrounged from backyards and
garages: stop signs, lawn-chairs, shipping-crates.
To perfect, propel summerlong, their
stylish *ollies, slides* and *aerials.*

Mornings colder now, their ramps grow
rococo, byzantine, composed of tiers
and balconies, bits of cars, teeter-totters,
weird rigging; their crashes more circus,
icarus, their tricks, soon-eclipsed, more and
more mannered, mannerist, *fin de siècle,*
leaps off a cliff.

LILACS

For two weeks their wanton odour
translates the town
into a seraglio–
Lilacs — an old word from the Persian
(my favorite words are Persian:
paradise, cinnamon, caravan, musk).

Two weeks of brazen thievery:
young couples bend the stalks and break off
the conical blossoms, lilac and white; children,
even old men, calmly stroll the avenues,
plumed, perfumed.

I breathe in their musk through the screen,
sitting here at my desk, at dusk,
the hour of thievery,
stealing words in bunches from the Persian:
tiger azure scarlet taffeta.
And more:
jasmine cashmere bazaar shawl.
From the street the couples' words
drift up to me: "Love me Love me;"
..."I'm yours forever"
While the lilacs whisper
insistently, "Take me Take me Take me."

ANTS AND PEONIES

In Eastern poetry, peony's
a metaphor
for feminine beauty.

They say ants crawl
on peonies each Spring,
to help them open —
tickling the bud,
licking the nectar —
you see them nibbling
at the swollen seams,
coaxing them to blossom,
let go.

But ants crawl on peonies
to collect free sugar —
that other's an old wives' tale.

Told by old wives
sitting by the fire,
musing on honeypots
and anthills.

FALL BULBS

Handful of bonemeal, cup of blood-
meal; palm's worth of peat moss,
and one of sheep shit. Stir
in a large bowl scooped in the earth.
Add water, and hair of the dog
culled from comb and brush, hoarded
in a drawer all summer like string —
an anti-enticement,
discouragement to squirrels.

Plug the bulbs into this hodgepodge
potage, and turn — give each a half-
twist, like a key in a lock. Put back
the earth more or less the way it was;
any stones that turn up
should be pocketed, and set
at the foot of the hedge.

Turn to stow the spade —
and already the concoction's cooking,
coddling, the bulbs mulling.
Simmering.

HER OWN TIME

for Karen

At the end of October
instead of turning her clocks back —
daylight savings to standard —
she declines. So fall and winter,
every time she checks the clock
(even the one in the car)
there's always this surprise,
this gift of a golden hour.
To finish a painting, a letter,
prepare supper; to be not forever
losing time, but gaining,
recovering time.
A zone her own.

Dark closes in so early these days —
nearing the end of the year —
but in all her rooms
a light shines:
there's always another hour.

MEMORY TREE II

for Mareika & Jesse

Karen sketches a Memory Tree
for her niece — a Wedding Tree,
Fingerprint Tree —
broad trunk, spreading branches,
and finally, at the twigs' fingertips,
leaves, where in a few weeks,
guests will press their thumbs.

A tree's memories
are recorded on scrolls
wound within the trunk's golden rings.

Sit sometimes, in the shade of this tree —
the leaves overhead
intricate signatures, ridges and whorls —
your memories reaching
as deep as its roots;
the boughs full of song.

GHOST FLOWER

After heavy summer rains
bell-shaped flowers
made of smoke and ashes
bloom in the forest —
their off-white flesh
waxy, cold
like flesh of the dead.

Feeding on roots
of nearby trees, in
deep shade they offer
their sour nectar to flies;
leaves, even stems off-white,
no green cells inside.

Ghost flowers linger
a few days, then wither away.
Pick one — it turns black,
secretes a clear liquid,
a few drops — as if its essence
three or four bitter tears.

MOTHS

Some moths — meal moths, flour moths —
fly in a haphazard manner
that makes them hard to catch;
this randomness
gradually selected itself.

Their relationship with lights
is widely misunderstood:
lights don't make moths demented,
suicidal, nor are they
"trying to get warm".
Moths navigate by the moon;
lured off course, revolving around
a streetlight, more and more are lost
as the loss of darkness intensifies. But,
as Kenneth Frank says in a recent *Discover*,
"Never argue against something
on behalf of moths."

A caterpillar, becoming somewhat frantic:
it's dusk — the pressure to find a place
to be alone, to pupate — the obscenity
of public metamorphosis, on a bus,
a fit, soiling yourself, drooling,
hurrying home
at the end of the day.
Or just the wish to rid yourself
of this pulpy larval body, walk naked
through the neighbourhood, dimly glowing.

The focus required; to shuck these dull habits,
needs that grab hold, like nicotine, down
inside your bones, cells.
To become not just someone,
but *something* else.

BED

Home's home. Your lair,
burrow. Your bed likes to
get messy like a desk — sheets/
rumpled papers overflowing —
you wrestle with these sheets
like Samson with his columns
crashing down on infidels —
wake Roman in your delirium,
wrapped around you like
a toga, you're wearing the bed,
it's become a cocoon you are
wrapped up inside, inside this
cold wintry house.

Spartans slept on stones like crows.

Soon you will wear this bed like
a diaper — an adult diaper —
you will never leave the bed, you
will wear it like a badge, you will
become the bed, sometimes calm
and tucked in, but mostly a mess.

GLUE-BOTTLE

September means mucilage: together
you return to school
— a new bottle —
sit and play with its red, rubbery tip
erect as a nipple, working it open
in your lap, pulling back the fleshy slit
like a half-closed eye; glistening.

Little man sleeping, his bleary peeper
lets slip one viscous tear.
This precious flask
in the corner of your desk —
color of urine — icon against
the winter ahead. His watery gaze:
your tedium.

STOVEPIPE

I'm in the kitchen in the old house
haunted house, grandma's farm
— she must have died. So I start
peeking around the room for her:
"come out, come out..." A stove-lid
pops up, "here I am! here I am!"
she shrieks — gasp of smoke
escaping from the oven.
The kettle whistles, screeches
"here I am," then whispers
in release: she speaks
in smoke and steam,
in the wind rising outside,
crying in the stovepipe.

You can feel the pressure building
like magma in a volcano,
her voice uncorkable unstoppable
unstopperable — I can't keep
a lid on it — playing hide-and-seek/
whack-a-mole/pop goes the weasel
with my grandmother's ghost
on an ash-grey winter morning.

FALSE SPRING

Citizens in shades and shirtsleeves
take to the streets — they've taken
off the gloves weeks ago, so
it's easy to spot those of us
with a shard of ice inside, still
bundled up in coats and boots.
Our heavy black clothes
our nakedness. Heads down
and full of endless lists:
"It's late, very late," we mutter
while sparrows dart about building nests,
tumble in the dust crying "Lechery!"

We recognize each other in the streets.
The old guys wrapped in greatcoats
all day in the library
thumbing through *Great Nudes of Western Art*,
making funny noises in the backs of their throats,
look up from their studies to nod to me.
And multi-layered Cassandra Baglady
at Queen and Regent, pauses
her harangue to bow as I go by,
offers me choicest cuts from her shopping-cart.
Beggars on corners don't nag,
even the civic shrubbery still swaddled
in burlap like Bible lepers or eremites
in hair-shirts, shudder in recognition as I pass.
Our dark clothes have become a habit —
we're kin, sisters, brothers who know
spring's fiction, the reality of winter.

WINTER'S FORMALITY

Everyone wears gloves in the formal snow
gloves, hats and boots.
A casual stroll? All who step out
stand at attention, their greetings
          jets of ice   stiff salutes.
(Note etiquette of narrow paths — who
walks ahead, who holds back.)
Everywhere, the solemn
parade-like pacing of an old garrison town.
A formality like geometry: each tiny front-
step lip and wide driveway's
underlined, cut out in bold caps:
"Beware of Falling Ice
and Snow (*chutes de glaçons*)!"

Winter goes on forever; a series
of late-night long-distance phone-calls
interrupts your sleep, the woman
on the other end can't speak —
you develop a fever, lose track
of the days more completely
with each passing storm.

Not another season but
another country — there are people
you run into only late on cold nights
wound in long scarves, only
their eyes are visible, still you stop
and recognize.
Or, you see their bundled shape, their
familiar steps ahead — someone from the old days,
someone you're sure died long ago.

NEW BEAT

I'm gonna move to a new town,
start wearing a Tyrolean hat
with a little shaving brush
of wild boar bristles on the brim.
Find a fresh set of pals;
they'll greet me each day
like a long-lost friend
with a new nickname
they've invented for me,
something like Pine-top or Jellyroll.

At night, cryptic magazines piled at my feet,
I'll sit beside a tiny radio
tuned to an atonal squawk.
Get in step
with the new shrewdness.

A FAVOUR FOR MARQUEZ

I'm wandering through the Superstore,
when an elegant South American gentleman
approaches me in *Frozen Foods;*
up close I realize it's Gabriel Garcia Marquez.
Politely, he asks a favour —
he needs a go-between, to buy and deliver tokens
to his beloved (a chocolate-coated ice cream,
exaggerated red flower) —
there's to be a concert under the stars tonight,
he wishes to accompany her there, but there's been
some sort of misunderstanding I can't make out,
(we're translating by idiom, not word for word).
I accept.

But right away, problems: due to the heat-wave,
the ice machine's broken down, customers press in,
demanding their treats,
but I flirt with the girl, and I'm lucky enough
to purchase the last one.
All the while, a small boy has been teasing me
about my mission — how seriously I take my goal
of placating the beautiful Mercedes.
There's a struggle, and a sort of exchange between us,
then he helps me find a rare orchid
in the jungle-like *Floral Department,*
and I set off through the pastel streets.

I arrive in the wrong neighbourhood, lost,
find myself down by the steaming river,
worried these large mosquitoes will infect me,
my feet stuck in the mud —
the boy appears and pulls me out,
and we approach Mercedes' apartment
in a red clay building in an old section of the city.
Now I see her, my love,

the girl from the ice-cream counter,
preparing for our date, I see her dress, mirror,
her make-up and scents, up close,
from angles only she can see,
and I realize I've become her, the beautiful,
the beloved,
yet still hurrying through the streets,
the boy by my side;
I look down at the gifts in my hands,
and now I become the ice cream, just about to melt,
the flower, trembling, just about to wither away...

ABOUT THE AUTHOR

Michael Pacey was born in Fredericton. He received his BA and BEd from the University of New Brunswick, his MFA, MA and PhD from the University of British Columbia. Pacey's first full-length collection of poetry, *The First Step,* was published by Signature Editions in 2011. His work has appeared in more than twenty literary magazines, including *The Malahat Review, The New Quarterly, Exile, Prairie Fire,* and *Descant.* He has also published a chapbook (*Anonymous Mesdemoiselles,* 1972), and a children's book (*The Birds of Christmas,* 1987). He was editor of *Prism International* and has taught at UBC and Lakehead University.

Eco-Audit

Printing this book using Rolland Opaque 30 instead of virgin fibres paper saved the following resources:

Solid Waste	Water	Air Emissions
20 kg	1,611 L	181 kg